The Mothers of Three Prophets

by
Jameelah Jones

Ta-Ha Publishers Ltd.
1, Wynne Road
London SW9 0BB

Reprinted 2003   2007

Published by

Ta-Ha Publishers Ltd.
1 Wynne Road
London SW9 0BB
UK

By: Jameelah Jones
General Editor: Afsar Siddiqui
Edited by: Abdassamad Clarke

British Library Cataloguing in Publication Data
Jones, Jameelah
Mothers of Three Prophets, The
I. Title

ISBN: 1 897940 22 X

Typeset by: BookWright, Isle of Lewis.

Printed By: DELUXE PRINTERS

For 5–10 years old

Contents

بسم الله الرحمن الرحيم

Introduction

Let's take a look at three mothers who played very important roles in the lives of their sons, sons chosen by Allah to be prophets. These women faced severe tests beyond the abilities of the average woman to endure. Each was inspired by Allah to be faithful, devoted and strong. These women took care of their sons, educated and prepared them for the task ahead. As far as we know, two of them struggled without the support of a husband. Here we will extend ourselves with the help of our imaginations to understand what they must have suffered.

The words for 'mother' are among the first that a human being utters. The Prophet was asked, *salla'llahu alaihi wa sallam*, "Who is most deserving of fine companionship?" He replied, "Your mother." He was asked again, "Then who next?" He replied, "Your mother." He was asked again, "Then who?" So he replied, "Your father, then your nearest relatives."

The first mother mentioned in this series is Hajar, the wife of Ibrahim and the mother of Ismail.

Hajars' Story

Long ago in the land which we now call Iraq, Ibrahim, *alaihi's-salaam*, the son of Azar, was sent as a prophet to guide people to the truth. He tried to guide them to stop worshipping idols and to worship Allah, the Creator.

Unfortunately, most of Ibrahim's people did not listen to him and did not benefit from his message. They turned away and insisted on doing what their fathers and mothers, and their grandfathers and grandmothers before them had done. Although Ibrahim brought clear proof, they stubbornly turned away.

So Ibrahim, peace be upon him, left them and migrated to Palestine. After living there awhile, one year there came a great drought. The land became very dry, grass and plant-life dried up, water disappeared and famine spread throughout the land. Once again Ibrahim decided to migrate. This time he went to Egypt.

He went to Egypt with his first wife, Sarah, who had come with him from Iraq. They lived in Egypt awhile, then returned to Palestine. This time Hajar accompanied them. The ruler of Egypt had given her to Sarah.

Sarah was barren. She had not been able to have children. This made her sad and she felt even sadder for her husband. She wanted to make him happy and so suggested that she give Hajar to him. Perhaps Allah would bless them with a child. Ibrahim accepted Sarah's suggestion. Before long, Hajar was expecting a child and soon had a baby boy. They named him Ismail.

It wasn't long, though, until Sarah began to feel jealous. Every time she looked at Hajar she remembered that she could not have a baby herself, and her jealousy increased. Finally, she spoke to Ibrahim about her feelings. She may have said something like, "Take this woman and her son away form here! Get her out of my sight! I can't live in the same house with her!" But we don't know the very words she spoke.

The prophet Ibrahim, peace be upon him, thought and thought about what to do. How could he separate himself from his wife and the son Allah had given him in his old age? And where could he take them? Maybe Sarah kept insisting and insisting. Perhaps she told Ibrahim again and again that she could not bear to live with Hajar and Ismail.

At last, Ibrahim, peace be upon him, was

shown the answer. Allah revealed to him that he should do as Sarah had asked. So, he gathered Hajar, Ismail and a few belongings and started travelling. They continued until they reached the land of *Hijaz* in Arabia. It is a barren place without much plant growth. It also had very few people at that time. Ibrahim was to leave Hajar and Ismail in that empty barren place.

Can you imagine how sad Hajar must have felt to be left alone with a nursing child in the midst of high bare mountains, lonely hills and empty, unfriendly, stony valleys? How many women can bear being alone, even in very safe places? But no people lived in this place at all.

Yet, Hajar really drew upon her faith and trust in Allah. When the prophet Ibrahim, peace be upon him, was about to set out again for Palestine, she caught hold of his sleeve and said, "Where are you going? Are you going to leave us all alone in this scary place?" She must have thought about what she would do when she ran out of food and water. How was she going to withstand the heat of the hot, hot sun?

Then she asked, "Did Allah tell you to do this? ... to leave us here?" Ibrahim said, "Yes." She bravely said, "Then He won't let us perish, He won't forsake us."

Ibrahim, peace be upon him, set out for Palestine, his heart full of concern for his wife and son.

He prayed:

"Our Lord! I have settled some of my children in an uncultivated valley near to Your Sacred House. Our Lord, that they may establish the prayer, so incline the hearts of people with yearning towards them and provide them with fruits in order that they may be thankful."

(*Surah Ibrahim* 14: 37).

After the he had left, Hajar looked around. All she could see were mountains and desert. She didn't see any water, plant life or places where humans might be living. Then she looked at her baby son and held on to him as if to say, "Do not worry little one and do not be afraid. I'm your mother and I will look after you, *insha'Allah*."

Hajar built a small shelter of twigs and desert bushes to shade them from the direct glare of the sun. They passed the day beneath it. When night came, Hajar and Ismail slept. Whenever she heard the slightest sound, whether a wild animal or the screech of a bird, she must have tightened her arms about her little son. Even the shifting of the winds would have been frightening in that strange and deserted place.

Days passed and the bits of food that she had brought with her ran out. Her breasts became dry and gave no milk for Ismail. They had no water to drink. Ismail was hungry and thirsty.

He began to cry. Hajar's heart almost broke from the concern she felt for her son. Tears ran down her face. She didn't know what to do.

Hours passed and the child's tears became more and more heart-wrenching for her. She thought that she could see the signs of death in his face. His voice began to weaken. She jumped up in alarm, placed Ismail on the ground and began desperately looking around, searching for water.

She ran up a hill, the one we know as *Safa*, to look as far as she could for water. But she couldn't see water anywhere. She couldn't see a living soul. So she ran down the hill again and clambered up *Marwa*, the hill just opposite to *Safa*. Again she scurried down from it and went up *Safa* again. She did this seven times until she had almost used up all her strength. She was afraid very much that Ismail would die. She raised her hands in prayer and begged Allah to help her.

Relief came. Allah provided for her and her son out of His infinite mercy. Ismail had been crying and beating the earth with his feet. Suddenly a spring of water began to flow beneath him. Hajar looked at the water and almost couldn't believe it. But, she ran to the water and gave some to her son, until his thirst was quenched. Then she drank until she was satisfied. This spring of water came from what we

know now as the well of *Zamzam*. Hajar sat with Ismail in her arms and thanked Allah for His mercy. She thanked Him for saving her son from perishing from thirst in the hot desert.

Birds began to fly over the place because of the water, hoping to drink. It so happened that the Jurhum tribe were passing in the desert and noticed the birds flying around and around. They knew at once that water must be there. When they came nearer, they saw Hajar sitting there with Ismail.

When they had met and talked together, they knew that there was something very special about this woman and her son and the well bubbling away in the middle of the stony desert. They asked Hajar to allow them to settle there with her, close to the well of *Zamzam*. She gave them permission because she felt she could trust them. Thus, Hajar lived among the tribe of Jurhum raising her son. She taught him and took care of him until he reached boyhood and was more and more able to care for himself.

Ibrahim, peace be upon him, did not forget Hajar and their son. He visited them after some time. On one of these visits, he said to his son, "I saw in a dream that I was sacrificing you, so consider what you think."

Ismail, peace be upon him, knew that his father was a prophet. He knew that the dreams of the prophets are true revelations from Allah. They are visions rather than what we call dreams.

He said, "O my father, do as you are commanded. You will find me, *insha'Allah*, one of the patient ones."

Ibrahim did not refuse to carry out what he thought was Allah's order to sacrifice his son. Likewise Ismail did not waver and did not disobey his father.

Once again Hajar faced an awful test. Her only son whom she had raised in such a difficult land was going to be sacrificed by his father. Perhaps Hajar sat down and recalled the day that Allah had rescued her and her son from dying of thirst by causing water to flow from beneath his feet. Glory be to Allah! Hajar was a believing, trusting woman. She could not even think of disobeying what she thought was Allah's order, even if it was that her only child be sacrificed.

Suddenly, as she waited for the terrible news, Ibrahim brought her instead great, good news. Allah had spared her son (He had never ordered that he should be sacrificed). Allah tells us in Qur'an:

"So when they had both submitted (their wills to Allah) and he (Ibrahim) had laid him prostrate on his forehead, We called out to him, 'O Ibrahim! You have already fulfilled the vision! In that way do We reward those who do right.'"

(*Surah as-Saffat* 37: 103-105)

Hajar was very happy because she had obeyed Allah's command. She was doubly happy because Ismail was safe.

So, Hajar lived with her son, looking after him and loving him until her death. At that time, Ismail had grown up to be a strong young man, well able to care for himself. And he was chosen by Allah to be a prophet, may Allah grant him peace. She had done her part in preparing him for his great task. It was Allah's will that the last prophet, Muhammad, the Seal of the Prophets, may Allah bless him and grant him peace, would be one of Ismail's descendants.

The Mother of Musa

The Pharaohs ruled Egypt long ago. They had come to hate the Children of Israel who had migrated to Egypt many years before during the time of the prophet Yusuf, *alaihi's-salaam.* The Pharaohs had turned the Children of Israel into slaves, making them build huge palaces and temples for them, and forcing them to work long hard hours without enough water or food.

One of the Pharaohs thought that he was god and that his people should worship him. One night he had a dream which almost frightened him to death. He called his astrologers, fortune-tellers and magicians together, and ordered them to tell him the meaning of his dream. One of them said, "A boy will be born among the Children of Israel. He will be your enemy and he will take your kingdom from you. He will bring another religion. He will not worship you, but will worship another god."

Pharaoh was so enraged by this prediction that he ordered that all baby boys among the Children of Israel should be killed, but the baby girls spared.

One night, not long after the Pharaoh's decree, an Israelite woman sat sadly in her home, thinking about the child she was carrying in her womb. The time of its birth was approaching nearer and nearer. What would she do if she had a boy? How could she save him from being murdered?

Pharaoh's army spread throughout the land, killing every baby boy born to every woman amongst the Children of Israel. People say that the number of baby boys murdered reached seventy thousand.

Finally the time for the baby's birth arrived. The mid-wife came to help. She delivered a son. As soon as the mid-wife looked on the face of the baby, her heart filled with compassion for it and she said, "Don't be afraid, I won't tell anyone." The little baby boy was Musa, peace be upon him.

Musa's mother hid him for a while, then she felt that Pharaoh's army were drawing near. She had an inspiration from Allah. Allah tells us in Qur'an:

> "And when We revealed to your mother that which was revealed, 'Cast (the child) into the chest and cast the chest into the river. The river will cast him up on the bank and an enemy to Me and an enemy to him will take

him up.' But I cast love over you (Musa) from Me and this in order that you might be reared under My eye."
(*Surah Taha* 20: 38-39)

So she nursed the child, then wrapped him up and put him in a chest which she let loose to float down the River Nile.

Her faith was severely tested. Worry and sadness almost made her lose her mind. As she watched the chest containing her little son rise and fall among the waves, her heart almost broke with pain. She watched until he floated from sight. However, her trust in Allah was real and firm, and she believed in His promise.

The waves carried the little baby Musa along until the chest reached a garden in the palace of the Pharaoh, which lay on the banks of the Nile. Some of the serving girls saw it and thought that it might contain something interesting so they carried it to their mistress Asiah, the wife of the Pharaoh.

Asiah opened the chest and what did she see? None other than a smiling baby boy. When the Pharaoh found out about the baby boy, of course he wanted to kill him. But his wife said, "Please don't kill him. Let him be our son. Let's take him as our son. Please let me have him." She kept begging and entreating the Pharaoh until he gave in and granted her wish. He didn't kill the baby Musa, who was the very one his dream was about, although he killed thousands of other babies who were no harm to him at all.

Meanwhile Musa's mother sat in her house, worried sick about Musa. She didn't know what had happened to him. She called her daughter Maryam and said to her, "Go and seek news of Musa. But be very careful and do not let anyone know what you are about."

Maryam went in search of news of Musa. She found out that he was right inside the Pharaoh's splendid palace, right in the middle of the royal family!

There in Pharaoh's palace Maryam watched as the wet-nurses, who had come to try and nurse the baby Musa, came and went. He would not accept the breast of any one of them. He simply refused to nurse.

Finally, Maryam said to Asiah, "I know an excellent wet-nurse. She is good and clean and all the babies love her. Do you want me to bring her to you? She is an excellent woman." However, she definitely did not tell Asiah that the woman was Musa's real mother, or even that she was her very own mother. Asiah agreed and sent messengers to fetch Musa's mother.

This story, Allah mentions in Qur'an too:

"And (O Musa) when your sister went forth and said, 'Shall I show you one who will nurse and rear the child?' So We brought you back to your mother that her eye might be cooled and so that she should not grieve." (*Surah Taha* 20: 40)

Musa's mother was really surprised when they came to request her presence at the palace. She couldn't believe that they wanted her to nurse a royal child. Her surprise was even greater when she realised that her son, whom she had cast into the river in a plain box, was alive and living in the Pharaoh's palace as the Queen's adopted son.

When Musa's mother entered the palace and saw her son, she almost burst with happiness and joy. Nonetheless she hid her emotions and appeared as though she did not know who the boy was. When she placed Musa at her breast, he accepted it and drank to his heart's content.

The Pharaoh and his household were astonished by this woman and the entire state of affairs. But they didn't know the secret nor did they understand what they had seen.

Asiah asked her to remain in the palace and be the baby's wet-nurse, but Musa's mother explained that she had other children at home and that she could not afford to leave them alone while she remained at the palace. So she said, "If you agree, I will take this child with me and nurse him and watch him until he is weaned and then I will return him to you."

Upon the insistence of Musa's mother, the

Queen agreed and gave Musa to her to take to her house. What else could she do? The baby would accept no-one else.

Musa's mother was delighted as she returned to her house with her son. She praised Allah and thanked Him for saving her son from being murdered or even drowned, and for returning him to her as she had been promised beforehand.

> "So We returned him to his mother to gladden her eyes, so that she would not be sad, and for her to know that the promise of Allah is true, but most of them do not know."
> (*Surah al-Qasas* 28: 13)

Allah entrusted Musa's mother with the upbringing and education of her son, after rescuing him from death at the hands of Pharaoh's soldiers – a fate which no other baby boy, born amongst the Children of Israel during that year, escaped.

Musa, peace be upon him, grew up among his brothers and sisters under the loving care of his mother, far away from fear and terror. As Allah made it happen, the very same person who had murdered untold numbers of infants in order to free himself of Musa was the very same person whom Allah made to shelter Musa. The Pharaoh fed, clothed, educated and protected him without knowing his secret. Yet, this was the very same boy who would grow up to be the man who would destroy Pharaoh and Pharaoh's religion.

After Musa was weaned, he returned to the palace and grew up in honour and respect. However, he was always near his mother's watchful eyes and in her compassionate heart. One day the command of Allah came and he had to leave Egypt, eventually to return as a prophet of his people, peace be upon him.

Musa, *alaihi's-salaam*, whose mother had cared for him, nurtured him and prepared him for manhood, had a great task before him. He was destined to lead the Children of Israel out of slavehood. His mother was one of those women who had been chosen by Allah and entrusted with the upbringing of one of the prophets of Allah.

Maryam, Mother of Isa

Hanna was the wife of Imran. She was a barren woman. She had not been able to bear children. Yet she yearned to have a child and to rejoice in it. It is said that one day she saw a bird feeding its young, so she prayed to Allah to grant her a child, and promised that she would dedicate the child to Allah's service.

After a while, Allah answered her prayer and she conceived. As the months passed, she felt the new life awakening inside her and her happiness overflowed. Allah had fulfilled her desire and given her a child in her old age. She thought much about the little boy who would carry on her husband's line. As her husband was also very old, Hanna was grateful indeed.

The moment for the birth arrived. Hanna was sorely disappointed. She had given birth to a girl. She was afraid that she would not be able to dedicate a daughter to the temple and to the service of Allah.

"And she said, 'Lord, I have given birth to a girl', and Allah knew best what she had given birth to. And the male is not like the female. 'And I have named her Maryam, and I seek refuge in You for her and her offspring from the accursed devil.'"

(*Surah Ali-Imran* 3: 36)

Allah had mercy on Hanna and accepted her promise that her child should be dedicated for service to Allah's House.

Hanna took her little girl to the temple in Jerusalem. She told the men who were worshipping there that she had brought her little girl because she had dedicated her to Allah's service.

All the men in the temple competed to become Maryam's guardian, but Zakariya, *alaihi's-salaam*, who was the prophet of that time, said to them, "I have the greatest right because my wife is her aunt." However, each of the men insisted that he be the guardian. So finally they settled the matter by drawing lots. All of them went to the river and threw their reed pens upon the water. He whose reed reached the bank successfully was to become the guardian of Maryam. They cast lots three times and Zakariya won each time. Allah says in Qur'an:

"And you were not among them when they cast lots to find out who should take care of Maryam. And you were not among them when they disputed."

(*Surah Ali-Imran* 3: 44)

Zakariya, peace be upon him, became Maryam's guardian and he built a room for her in the upper levels of the temple. He served her faithfully and made sure that her needs were fulfilled. In this way, Maryam grew up in a small niche, worshipping Allah in devotion and submission, in fulfillment of her mother's promise.

One day, Zakariya, peace be upon him, entered her room and was amazed to see food in the room which he had not brought to her. He asked her in amazement, "Where did you get this from, Maryam? Who brought this to you?" He knew that Maryam was in such a place that no-one came to visit her.

Allah says in Qur'an:

"Right graciously did her Lord accept her and He made her grow in purity and beauty. Zakariya undertook to take care of her. Every time he entered her chamber to see her, he found her supplied with food."
He said, "Maryam, where did you get this?"
She said, "It is from Allah. Surely Allah provides for whom He will without measure."
(*Surah Ali-Imran* 3: 37)

After that, whenever Zakariya went into Maryam's room, he found food already there. During summer, she had fruit which normally is found in winter. During winter she had fruit which is normally found in summer. Zakariya, peace be upon him, realised that Allah had favoured Maryam and raised her above other worshippers.

Zakariya, *alaihi's-salaam,* was so affected by Maryam's devotion and faith that, right away, he prayed to Allah and asked Him to give him a child in his old age. He prayed:

"O my Lord! Give me from You pure offspring. Truly, You are the One Who hears prayer."

(*Surah Ali-Imran* 3: 38)

Maryam spent her time worshipping and remembering Allah in complete submission to Him. One day, while she was praying, an angel appeared before her. The angel had taken the form of a human being. Maryam said:

"I seek refuge in the All-Merciful from you, (come no nearer) if you fear Allah."

She appealed to him not to invade her privacy.

However, he had been sent by Allah, so he said to her:

"I am only a messenger of your Lord to give you the gift of a pure son."

She said, "How shall I have a son, seeing that no man has touched me and I am not unchaste?"

He said, "That is what your Lord said, 'It is easy for Me, and so that We can make him a sign for people and a mercy from Us.'"

(*Surah Maryam* 19: 18-21)

One can only imagine how Maryam must have felt. She became pregnant. It has been said that once her clothes became tight for her, she secluded herself from people and went off to be alone until the moment arrived for her to give birth.

At that time, she leaned against a date-palm and said:

"I wish that I had died before this and that I had been someone forgotten."

She didn't have anyone to help her at a time when a woman most needs help. However, Allah was with her and He is the best One to help. He says, in Qur'an:

But (a voice) cried to her from beneath it (the palm-tree), "Grieve not! For your Lord has provided beneath you a small river. And shake towards yourself the trunk of the palm-tree, it will let fresh ripe dates fall upon you. So eat and drink and cool (your) eye. And if you see any of mankind then say, 'I have vowed to the All-Merciful a fast, so I will not speak on this day to any human being.'"

(*Surah Maryam* 19: 24-26)

After giving birth, Maryam carried her son back to her village. The people were astonished when they saw her. Some screamed in her face, and some felt sorry for her and said:

"O Maryam, you have brought an amazing thing. O sister of Haroun, your father was not an evil man nor was your mother indecent!" (*Surah Maryam* 19: 28)

Maryam did not answer theme because of the fast she had been told to observe. She only pointed to the baby as if to say, "Ask him!" They were even more astonished.

They said, "How can we talk to one who is a child in the cradle?"

Nevertheless, their answer came from the mouth of Maryam's baby.

He said, "Truly, I am the slave of Allah. He has given me the Book (of revelation) and made me a prophet." (*Surah Maryam* 19: 30)

They were really astounded by all of this and believed that the entire situation was indeed miraculous, and it was. They believed that the baby's speaking was a true sign of Maryam's innocence and purity of character.

However, some of the people who were not there when the baby spoke thought that this was a trick which Maryam's family had thought of to hide her guilt. They slandered her because they could not accept the truth. In spite of this, Maryam lived among them with no other anxiety than raising her son to be a good person. She met their doubting eyes secure in Allah's promise.

When her son, Isa, *alaihi's-salaam*, was old enough to be educated, she sent him to some teachers. He was soon known to be an intelligent boy of the finest character. When the Jews became aware of his presence among them, they were afraid of him and plotted against him. For this reason, his mother fled with him to Egypt.

There, he completed his education, and when he was twelve or thirteen years of age, she returned with him to Palestine, to a small village near Jerusalem. She always watched him carefully and guarded him from hostile Jews, as much as she could, until he reached thirty years of age. At this time revelation came to him. He was informed that the time had come to assume the mantle of prophethood. He had been chosen by Allah to be a prophet and a messenger to the Children of Israel.

When Maryam saw this and recognised that her son, for whom she had struggled and taken the blame of her people, had come of age, she was extremely happy. Her heart fairly leapt for joy. She gave her son her blessing and told him that she had known all along that he was going to be a prophet. She told him that Allah had informed her of this before he was born and that he, himself, had spoken to the people of this when he was just in the cradle. She told Isa to go and call the people to the worship of Allah and to spread His word. So Isa, peace be upon him, left his mother for the path of Allah after being cared for and cherished by her for thirty years.

Allah says the following about the prophet Isa, *alaihi's-salaam*, in the Qur'an:

"He has made me kind to my mother and not overbearing or disobedient."
(*Surah Maryam* 19: 32)

Allah has the following to say about Maryam:
"And Maryam, the daughter of Imran, who guarded her private parts, so We breathed into it of Our spirit and she affirmed the truth of the words of her Lord and of His revelations and was one of the devout."
(*Surah At-Tahrim* 66: 22)